)

Massachusetts
Facts and Symbols

by Emily McAuliffe

Consultant:
Mary Ellen Sorensen
President
Massachusetts Council for the Social Studies

Hilltop Books
an imprint of Franklin Watts
A Division of Grolier Publishing
New York   London   Hong Kong   Sydney
Danbury, Connecticut

Hilltop Books
http://publishing.grolier.com

Library of Congress Cataloging-in-Publication Data
McAuliffe, Emily.
  Massachusetts facts and symbols/by Emily McAuliffe.
  p.cm.—(The states and their symbols)
  Includes bibliographical references and index.
  Summary: Presents information about the state of Massachusetts and its nickname,
motto, and emblems.
  ISBN 0-7368-0082-4
  1. Emblems, State—Massachusetts—Juvenile literature. [1. Emblems, State—
Massachusetts. 2. Massachusetts.] I. Title. II. Series: McAuliffe, Emily. States and their
symbols.
CR203.M39M33 1999
974.4—dc21
                                                                98-3674
                                                                CIP
                                                                AC

Editorial Credits
Mark Drew, editor; James Franklin, cover designer and illustrator; Sheri Gosewisch,
  photo researcher

Photo Credits
Eliot Cohen, 6
One Mile Up Inc., 8, 10 (inset)
Robert McCaw, cover, 12, 14, 16
Unicorn Stock Photos/Andre Jenny, 10; Jean Higgins, 18; Charles E. Schmidt, 20;
  Arthur Gurmankin, 22 (top & bottom); Arthur Gurmankin & Mary Morina, 22
  (middle)

Table of Contents

Fast Facts about Massachusetts

Capital: Boston is the capital of Massachusetts.

Largest City: Boston is the largest city in Massachusetts. More than 500,000 people live in Boston.

Size: Massachusetts covers 10,555 square miles (27,337 square kilometers).

Location: Massachusetts is in the northeastern United States.

Population: 6,117,520 people live in Massachusetts (U.S. Census Bureau, 1997 estimate).

Statehood: Massachusetts became the sixth state on February 6, 1788.

Natural Resources: Massachusetts has stone, lumber, and fish.

Manufactured Goods: Workers in Massachusetts make computers, machinery, and paper.

Crops: Farmers in Massachusetts raise cranberries, vegetables, and cattle.

Settlers named Massachusetts after the Massachusett group of Native Americans. The Massachusett lived near what is now Great Blue Hill. This hill is in the eastern part of the state. The word Massachusetts means great hill place.

Massachusetts has many nicknames. Some people call it the Bay State or Old Bay State. These names honor the Massachusetts Bay. This bay borders some of the state's eastern coast. The Massachusetts Bay is part of the Atlantic Ocean.

People also call Massachusetts the Pilgrim State. The Pilgrims were settlers from England. English rulers would not let the Pilgrims practice their religion. So they left England and sailed to America on the *Mayflower*. The Pilgrims founded Plymouth Colony in Massachusetts in 1620.

Another nickname for Massachusetts is the Old Colony State. This name honors Plymouth Colony.

The Massachusetts Bay borders some of the state's eastern coast.

State Seal and Motto

Massachusetts adopted its state seal in 1885. The state seal is a symbol. It reminds people in Massachusetts of their state's government. The state seal also makes government papers official.

The Massachusetts coat of arms appears in the center of the state seal. The coat of arms shows a Native American man holding a golden bow and arrow. The arrow points downward to show that he is peaceful. This suggests that Massachusetts is a peaceful state.

A white star is next to the Native American man's head. The star means that Massachusetts was one of the 13 colonies.

The Massachusetts state motto also appears on the seal. A motto is a word or saying that people believe in. The state motto is "Ense petit placidam sub libertate quietem." This is Latin for "By the sword we seek peace, but peace only under liberty."

Massachusetts adopted its state seal in 1885.

State Capitol and Flag

The Massachusetts capitol building is in Boston. Boston is the capital of Massachusetts. People in Massachusetts call the capitol the State House. Government officials work in the State House. They meet there to make the state's laws.

Workers built the State House from 1795 to 1798. The State House is brick. The roof has a rounded part called a dome. A layer of gold covers the wooden dome.

The State House stands on what was once John Hancock's cow pasture. John Hancock was the first person to sign the Declaration of Independence. This official paper announced the independence of the 13 colonies. John Hancock also was the first governor of Massachusetts.

The Massachusetts government adopted the state flag in 1971. The flag is white. The state coat of arms appears in the center of the flag.

The State House is in Boston.

State Bird

The black-capped chickadee is the Massachusetts state bird. The Massachusetts state government chose this bird in 1941. Many black-capped chickadees live in Massachusetts.

People call these birds chickadees because of their song. Chickadees sound like they say "chickadee-dee-dee" when they sing.

Adult chickadees are five to six inches (13 to 15 centimeters) long. The tops of their heads are black. This is why people call them black-capped chickadees.

Many chickadees build small nests in trees or tree stumps. Some build nests in fence posts. Chickadees make their nests out of grass and feathers. Female chickadees lay six to eight eggs in their nests. The eggs are white with red-brown spots.

Many black-capped chickadees live in Massachusetts.

State Tree

The state tree of Massachusetts is the American elm. It became the state tree in 1941.

Massachusetts chose the American elm to honor a historical event. George Washington took command of the Continental army in Massachusetts. This army fought against Great Britain during the Revolutionary War (1775–1783). Washington stood under an American elm when he took command.

American elms can grow to be 65 to 100 feet (20 to 30 meters) tall. Some American elms reach 120 feet (37 meters) tall. They have gray bark and dark green leaves. The leaves are oval shaped.

Wood from elm trees is very strong. It does not split easily. People build furniture from elm wood.

American elms have gray bark and oval leaves.

State Flower

The mayflower became the Massachusetts state flower in 1918. Some people believe the Pilgrims named this flower after their ship.

Mayflowers bloom in spring. They have five pink or white petals. Petals are the colored outer parts of flowers.

Mayflowers grow well in wooded areas. They grow close to the ground. People also call the mayflower the ground laurel.

Many mayflowers once grew in Massachusetts. Today, mayflowers are not as plentiful. People dug up too many mayflower plants. In 1925, the Massachusetts government decided to save the mayflower. People may pick mayflowers growing on public land. But they can no longer dig up mayflower plants.

Mayflowers have five pink or white petals.

State Horse

Massachusetts adopted the Morgan as the state horse in 1970. The first Morgan was born in West Springfield, Massachusetts. His name was Figure. No one knows exactly when Figure was born. Some people think it was around 1789. People named Morgans after Figure's owner. His name was Justin Morgan.

Morgans are small, strong horses. Adult Morgans are 57 to 62 inches (145 to 157 centimeters) tall. They weigh 900 to 1,100 pounds (408 to 499 kilograms). Morgans are red-brown, brown, or black. Some Morgans are bay colored. Bay-colored horses are red-brown and have black legs, tails, and manes.

Morgans are calm and smart. They make excellent work horses. They also make good riding horses. Morgans are a popular type of police horse.

Morgans are small, strong horses. They make excellent work horses.

State Dog: The Boston terrier has been the state dog since 1979. Boston terriers are native to Massachusetts.

State Marine Mammal: The right whale became the state marine mammal in 1980. Right whales swim off the coast of Massachusetts.

State Fish: The cod became the Massachusetts state fish in 1974. Cod fishing is an important business in Massachusetts.

State Beverage: Cranberry juice has been the state beverage since 1970. Cranberries are an important crop in Massachusetts.

State Dessert: Boston cream pie is the state dessert. Massachusetts school children selected it in 1996.

State Cookie: The state cookie is the chocolate chip cookie. Massachusetts chose it in 1997. Ruth Wakefield invented the chocolate chip cookie in Whitman, Massachusetts.

The Boston terrier is the state dog of Massachusetts.

Places to Visit

Plimoth Plantation

Plimoth Plantation is in the town of Plymouth. Visitors to the plantation see how the Pilgrims lived. They also may board the *Mayflower II*. This ship is a copy of the *Mayflower*. The Pilgrims sailed to America on the *Mayflower* in 1620.

New England Aquarium

The New England Aquarium is in Boston. It is one of the most famous aquariums in the nation. More than 2,000 types of sea animals live there. Aquarium visitors see penguins, seals, sharks, and fish.

Cape Cod National Seashore

The Cape Cod National Seashore is a national park in eastern Massachusetts. The seashore has 43,556 acres (17,627 hectares) of shoreline. Visitors swim in the Atlantic Ocean. They hike on the 10 nature trails. Visitors also take guided canoe tours during summer.

Words to Know

bloom (BLOOM)—to flower

coat of arms (KOHT UHV ARMZ)—a drawing usually in the shape of a shield that often has other figures around it; a coat of arms stands for a family, city, or state.

dome (DOHM)—a rounded part of a roof

motto (MOT-oh)—a word or saying that people believe in

petals (PET-uhlz)—the colored outer parts of flowers

Pilgrims (PIL-gruhmz)—a group of settlers who sailed to America from England in 1620

symbol (SIM-buhl)—something that stands for or suggests something else; the U.S. flag is a symbol of the United States.

Read More

Bock, Judy and Rachel Kranz. *Scholastic Encyclopedia of the United States.* New York: Scholastic Inc., 1997.

Capstone Press Geography Department. *Massachusetts.* One Nation. Mankato, Minn.: Capstone Press, 1996.

George, Jean Craighead. *The First Thanksgiving.* New York: Philomel Books, 1993.

Warner, J. F. *Massachusetts.* Hello U.S.A. Minneapolis: Lerner Publications, 1994.

Useful Addresses

Secretary of the Commonwealth of Massachusetts
220 Morrissey Boulevard
Boston, MA 02133

State Library of Massachusetts
State House
24 Beacon Street
Boston, MA 02133

Internet Sites

Massachusetts Facts
http://www.state.ma.us/sec/cis/cismaf/mafidx.htm
New England Aquarium
http://www.neaq.org/index.html
Plimoth Plantation
http://pilgrims.net/plimothplantation/vtour/index.htm

Index